HOW TO USE OUR B(

Coloring Fun Let your child's imagination run wild as they color in the simple hockey items and scenes. Encourage them to experiment with different colors and techniques.

Storytelling Create stories together based on the scenes in the book. Ask your child to imagine what's happening in the picture and what the players might be saying to each other..

Practice Fine Motor Skills Coloring is a great way for children to develop their fine motor skills and hand-eye coordination. Encourage them to stay within the lines for a neat finish.

Display Artwork Show off your child's masterpieces by hanging them on the fridge or in their room. You can also take photos of their artwork to share with family and friends.

Relaxation Time Coloring can be a calming activity for both children and adults. Spend some quiet time together coloring and unwinding after a busy day.

NOAH & Lucy
PUBLISHING

Free Digital Coloring pages!

RECEIVE FREE COLORING PAGES FOR YOU & YOUR LITTLES EACH MONTH WHEN YOU VISIT & JOIN OUR FACEBOOK GROUP!

Share your creations in our facebook group to show others how you are using our books!
Scan the QR code to join!

FOLLOW US

NOAH & Lucy
PUBLISHING

THANK YOU FOR YOUR PURCHASE!

THIS BOOK BELONGS TO:

TAKE CARE OF YOURSELF

THANK YOU FOR YOUR PURCHASE!

CONNECT WITH US:

Terms of Use

CHECK OUT OUR OTHER TITLES FOR MORE EDUCATIONAL FUN!

Made in United States
Troutdale, OR
09/10/2024

22723210R00051